rats

understanding and
caring for your pet

Written by
Julia Smith
Additional material by Alison Triggs

rats

understanding and
caring for your pet

Written by
Julia Smith
Additional material by Alison Triggs

Magnet & Steel Ltd

www.magnetsteel.com

Every reasonable care has been taken in the compilation of this publication. The Publisher and Author cannot accept liability for any loss, damage, injury or death resulting from the keeping of rats by user(s) of this publication, or from the use of any materials, equipment, methods or information recommended in this publication or from any errors or omissions that may be found in the text of this publication or that may occur at a future date, except as expressly provided by law.

No animals were harmed in the making of this book.

The 'he' pronoun is used throughout this book instead of the rather impersonal 'it', however no gender bias is intended.

Printed and Bound in China

ISBN: 978-1-907337-09-3
ISBN: 1-907337-09-1

Contents

Pictured:
Black Berkshire

Perfect pets

Rats are more usually thought of as perfect pests rather than perfect pets, but the domestic rat is a very different animal from its wild ancestors.

- For the last 100 years or more, rats have been selectively bred to be pets. They have a much more placid temperament and look much more attractive than their wild cousins.

- Rats are highly intelligent, and so they make interesting and entertaining pets.

- A rat is capable of forming a close bond with his human owner, and rat enthusiasts claim their pets show dog-like loyalty and devotion.

- The domestic rat is a naturally clean animal, and if the normal hygiene procedures are followed – needed when handling all small animals – there is minimal risk of a pet rat spreading disease.

- If you provide a suitably stimulating environment, a rat will exercise himself – so this is a pet that is suitable for people of all ages.

Pictured:
Black Hooded Rat

- A rat needs to spend quality time with his owner but you can devise a routine which will suit your lifestyle. This means that the rat is a perfect pet for those who go out to work.

- Over the years enthusiasts have developed different coat colours and markings for rats, which means there is plenty of choice available. You may even decide to show your rat in a competition!

Special requirements

The domestic rat is a tough little creature. He is easy to care for, he is not a fussy feeder, and, with good management, he will suffer few health problems. However, like all living animals, he has his own special needs, of which you need to be aware.

- The rat is a born problem solver, and this means that he may put his energies into becoming a great escape artist. Regardless of the type of accommodation you provide, security is paramount.

- Rats are lively and inquisitive and will not thrive without occupation. You need to provide toys and play equipment in his cage, otherwise your rat will become bored and destructive.

- A rat should be given at least one hour outside his cage every day so he can exercise and explore. But make sure that he cannot escape!

- Rats can also be predatory, so be careful if you keep other small animals, such as mice and birds.

- Rats are social animals and will be miserable if they are kept on their own. You should keep at least a pair of rats (same sex) or, even better, a small group.

- The ancestors of domestic rats are crepuscular which means they are most active around dawn and dusk.

- The domestic rat will relate closely with his human family, but handling from an early age is essential so that he understands the manners that are required of him.

- There is no point in keeping a small animal as a pet unless you want to spend time with him. This is particularly important with the domestic rat, which learns to become reliant on human company.

- Although rats are low maintenance pets, you still need to keep a regular check on them and their cage will need cleaning on a regular basis.

- If you go away on holiday, you will need to make suitable arrangements for your pets – either taking them to a fellow rat-keeper, or getting someone to come in and look after them.

Where do rats come from?

Pictured:
Black Roan

Where do rats come from?

The rat is a member of the rodent family, which is a huge group of mammals with over 2,000 different species that live in habitats all over the world.

The one feature that all rodents have in common is their exceptional ability to gnaw. They get their name from the Latin word 'rodere' which means 'to gnaw'. They are all equipped with four large teeth, called incisors, which keep growing throughout an animal's lifetime.

There are 80 species of rats that live in a wide range of environments around the world. They include the South American fish-eating rat, the kangaroo rat from North America, and the African spiny tree rat. However, there are two species that are most closely associated with human history – the black rat (rattus rattus) and the brown or Norwegian rat (rattus Norvegicus).

Our domestic rat is directly descended from the brown rat. It is thought that both the brown rat and the black rat originated in Asia. It was as a result of their special skills at living among human populations, and travelling with people as stowaways in ships, that led to their spread across the world.

The black rat is the smaller of the two species, generally measuring 16- 22cm (7- 9in) in length, with a tail of 17- 24cm (7- 10in). He is grey-black in colour and tends to live above ground. He is known for his climbing skills and will often make his home the upper levels of buildings. He is also known as the 'roof rat' and the 'ship rat'. The black rat is basically a plant eater, but, like all rats, he is a natural scavenger and will eat anything that comes his way.

Plague rats

It is the black rat that is responsible for giving the species a bad name; he was host for the bubonic plague, also known as the Black Death, which claimed some 200 million lives. The first major outbreak occurred in Europe in the 6th century, but it was during the Medieval period that the plague became pandemic. Starting in China in 1328, its spread across the globe was relentless, and by 1350 it was estimated that a third of the world's population had died.

Rats are blamed for spreading the plague.

In fact, it was not the rats themselves, but the fleas carried on the rats that were responsible for the spread of disease. Other animals also carried these fleas, and the poor state of hygiene was also a highly significant factor. However, the blame ended up with the black rat, and it is one of the reasons why rats are still feared by many people.

Sewer rats

The brown rat is larger than the black rat,
measuring 22- 26cm (9- 11in) in length, with a tail
of 18- 22cm (7- 9in). Most are grey-brown in colour,
and they live in underground burrows and tunnels.
The brown rat is a very good swimmer, and can even
swim underwater for short periods. It is because of
this particular skill that brown rats have made their
home in sewers, and are often known as 'sewer rats'.

Brown rats prefer to eat grain and carrion meat, but
their success as a species is due to their ability to
survive wherever people live, scavenging on all types
of food and rubbish. They are nocturnal, so they are
mostly active at night when there is least danger
from people and from predators.

In areas where brown and black rats inhabit the
same territory, the larger brown rat will drive
the black rat away, and so the urban brown rat
has triumphed in terms of numbers, due to its
tremendous versatility and adaptability.

Pictured:
This is an Agouti

Lucky rats

In some countries, the rat has thrown off his bad reputation and is even seen as a symbol of good luck. The Chinese astrological cycle begins with the rat, and those born under this sign are thought to be quick-witted, clever at business, and loyal to their families.

In India, rats are believed to be representatives of the Hindu goddess, Karniji, and in a village in Deshnok a temple is specially dedicated to them. It is estimated that 10,000 brown rats live in the temple, sharing food with worshippers and even eating from the same plates. The people of Deshnok believe they will be reincarnated as rats when they die.

Predators

In the wild, there are a number of predators that will attack rats. Snakes are probably their greatest enemy, but they also face danger from the skies in the shape of owls, hawks and eagles.

In an urban setting, a rat has most to fear from humans and the poisons that are laid down in an effort to reduce their ever-growing populations. Cats and dogs may also attack rats, which is why great care must be taken if you have a multi-animal household.

Breeding rats

The spread of rats worldwide is truly phenomenal; it is reckoned that there are as many rats living in cities as there are people. New York has an estimated rat population of 96 million.

One of the principal reasons for these incredible statistics is the rat's reproductive cycle. A female brown rat (doe) may have up to seven litters a year. The average litter size is eight, but a doe may have up to 22 babies, known as kittens, in one litter. Pregnancy lasts for 21- 23 days, and when the kittens are born they are virtually helpless. They have no fur; they are blind and cannot hear. All they can do is suckle milk from their mother.

Snakes are the rat's natural enemies.

However, their growth rate is truly amazing. Within a couple of weeks they can hear and see and will be running around. At three to four weeks the young rats are fully weaned and independent. By the time rats are five to six weeks old, they are sexually mature and ready to start breeding.

Life may be action packed from an early age, but rats have a short life expectancy. On average a wild rat will live for just 12 months. Fortunately, the domestic rats we keep as pets have a better life expectancy and will generally reach over two years of age.

The record for the oldest rat goes to Rodney, a laboratory rat, who lived to the grand old age of seven years and four months.

It is the rat's amazing adaptability coupled with its rapid breeding cycle that has made the species so successful.

The human link

The human link

In the early 1800s, Europe was teeming with rats, and this gave rise to a new sport – rat baiting.

People were paid money to catch rats, which were to be used in hectic gambling sessions. A big earth pit was dug, rats were released and bets were laid on how many rats a dog could kill.

This sport became so popular that the best ratting dogs were selectively bred, and this resulted in many of the dog breeds we know today, including Yorkshire Terriers, Manchester Terriers and Black and Tan Terriers.

In 1835 the Cruelty to Animals Act was passed in the UK, which banned baiting with bulls and bears, but rat baiting continued to flourish for many decades. At one time, there were 70 rat pits in London alone.

Rat catchers

The large numbers of wild rats meant that some efforts were made to try to control the population. Rat catchers were appointed, and one man, Jack Black, who was rat catcher to Queen Victoria, is responsible for the start of keeping rats as pets.

When Jack Black came across some oddly-coloured rats, he bred them and, in time he had a range of colours including, black, albino, fawn and grey, as well as particolours, which he sold as pets. This was the start of breeding rats selectively as pets, with the aim of producing different colours and a calmer, more laid back temperament.

Rats as food

In most countries there is a strong taboo against eating rats, mostly because of their association with the spread of disease, and there are also religious prohibitions in some cultures. However, there are notable exceptions. The Hawaiians and Polynesians use rats as a source of food, and in the Philippines, ricefield rats are included in the diet. In South East Asia, bandicoot rats are eaten, and the Musahar community in northern India farm rats for food on a commercial basis.

Pictured:
British Blue

Laboratory rats

Towards the end of the 19th century, people found another use for the ever-present rat population. Scientists took wild brown rats and bred them in captivity to use for scientific experiments. They found them easy to keep and their rapid growth and reproduction rate made them the perfect subjects for research.

Occasionally albino rats appeared and, over many generations, the laboratory rat became quite distinct from the wild brown rat.

The practice of experimenting on rats has continued to the present day, and they have played a part in the advances made in genetics, the effects of drugs and the treatment of disease. As rats are so intelligent, they have also been used in studies of mental processes, group living, and the effects of overcrowding.

Pictured:
Pink-eyed White

The rat fancy

Following on from Jack Black came Mary Douglas, who is known as the 'mother' of the rat fancy. By the end of the 19th century, coloured mice were being exhibited at shows and in 1895 the National Mouse Club was formed in England. Mary was keen that the domestic rats, kept as pets, should also be recognised and through her work, the first show classes for fancy rats were held in 1901. In 1912, due to the growing interest in keeping fancy rats, the club's name was changed to the National Mouse and Rat Club.

Mary Douglas died in 1921, and, without her campaigning zeal, the rat fancy almost faded from existence. In 1929, the name 'Rat' was dropped from the national club and over the next 45 years interest in rat keeping was sporadic.

All this changed in 1976 when the National Fancy Rat Society was formed. This was the first 'rats only' organisation, and, from that time onwards, a growing number of rat enthusiasts have been breeding them and showing them, and their popularity as pets has soared.

In the USA, there is little documentary evidence of keeping rats as pets. They were certainly used in laboratories in the early 20th century, and it seems that breeders supplied laboratories and also sold some as pets.

Pictured:
Black Hooded
specimen

The breakthrough came in 1978 with the establishment of the Mouse and Rat Breeders Association, followed in 1983 by the American Fancy Rat and Mouse Association. The fancy grew with the help of imports from the UK, and before long American rat enthusiasts were starting their own breeding programmes and developing new colours and varieties. In the last 15 years, more and more people have discovered that rats make perfect pets, and the domestic rat – now so far removed from his wild cousin – is a firm favourite.

The rat's world

The rat's world

The rat is a fascinating creature, superbly adapted to survive in a wide range of environments. What is it that makes the rat so special?

Body

The rat has a relatively long, racy body measuring 15- 25cm (6- 10in), with the tail slightly shorter than the body itself. The buck (male) is bigger than the doe (female). Typically he will weigh up to 700g (1lb 8oz) – half as much again as the female.

Tail

The rat has a furless, snake-like tail. This may not look attractive, but it serves two very important functions. Firstly, it is used to regulate body temperature. The tail, which is covered in fine bristles, contains many blood vessels; if a rat gets too hot, the blood vessels swell, allowing warm blood to flow through the tail.

Pictured:
Black Berkshire. If you watch a rat climbing you will see that it is his tail that aids his balance.

The warm blood loses heat through the surface of the tail and returns to the body at a lower temperature. Conversely, if a rat gets too cold the blood vessels constrict, minimising the blood flow to the tail and, thus, conserving body heat.

Secondly, the rat uses his tail to balance, and this gives him the ability to climb over any obstacle, scaling great heights, using anything he finds – ropes, chains, branches, and even telephone wires.

Feet

The rat's feet are covered with fine hair; the toes have strong nails which are used for burrowing. The toes are flexible, which gives the rat the dexterity he needs to climb, to investigate, and to scavenge.

Teeth

Rats have two types of teeth. The all-important incisors are the four long, sharp, front teeth that are used for gnawing. There are two on the top jaw and two on the bottom jaw. They grow throughout a rat's life – up to to 12cm (5in) in the course of a year. In addition, a rat has 12 molars (six on the top jaw, six on the bottom) which are used for grinding food prior to swallowing. These do not continue to grow and are not replaced – they must last the duration of a rat's lifetime.

Coat

The standard coat for a rat has two layers: the topcoat consists of long guard hairs, which are waterproof, and the soft, dense undercoat acts as insulation. Breeders have now developed a curly rex coat, and also a hairless variety of rat (see page 55).

The senses

The rat has finely-tuned senses which allow him to find food and shelter, and to sense danger.

Sight

A rat's vision is inferior to our own, and is the least important of his senses as he is far more reliant on smell and touch.

The rat sees in ultra violet colours – blues and greens – and his vision is quite blurry, especially more than a few feet away from him.

Hearing

Rats have an acute sense of hearing – much better than our own – and can pick up soft sound and high frequencies, going into the range of ultrasound.

Pictured:
The rat is mostly active in low light so he relies on his sense of smell and touch rather than his eyesight.

Smell

Rats perceive the world primarily through their sense of smell, which is far superior to ours. They use their noses to find food and to detect possible danger, but their sense of smell is also of great importance when communicating with each other. Rats recognise each other by scent. Urine marking, which is mostly carried out by bucks, but also by does when they are coming into season, carries a host of useful information.

By scenting drops of urine, a rat can tell the sex of the individual, if this is a female, whether she is sexually receptive, whether he/she is a stranger or known to him, the status of the animal (dominant or subordinate), and even the stress level of the individual concerned.

Touch

The rat uses the pads on his feet to assess the terrain, but it is his whiskers that provide detailed sensory information. As a rat investigates, be whisks his whiskers back and forth, dozens of times a second. They brush over floors, walls, obstacles, food, and other rats, sending detailed messages to his brain. From these, a rat is able to build up a detailed picture of his environment, which may be of even greater significance than our own visual perceptions.

Pictured:
The rat uses his whiskers to explore the environment.

Rat behaviour

The rat is a social animal that has always lived in large groups. As a result, he has evolved sophisticated methods of communicating with fellow rats. As pet owners we need to read our rats' body language, and pick up on the sounds they make, so we can understand their feelings and intentions.

Standing upright

A rat will stand on his hind legs, nose lifted and whiskers twitching, when something has caught his attention. He will also be using his acute sense of hearing to find out what is going on.

Swaying

Owners have observed rats swaying from side to side, and this has been most frequently observed in albino rats. It is thought that this may an attempt to focus better on a distant object, particularly if the rat is about to jump. As albino rats have poorer vision than rats of other colours, they are more likely to be seen doing this.

Pictured:
Black Roan

Tail swishing

You may see a rat wagging or swishing his whole tail, or just twitching the tip. This is a sign of tension or excitement, and is most likely to be seen prior to an aggressive encounter if a rat spots a predator.

Play fighting

By the time they are around 18 days old, baby rats will spend increasing amounts of time play fighting. They chase each other and try to pin each other to the ground. The aim seems to be to get at the nape of the neck; if this is achieved, the victor gently nuzzles his opponent with his snout.

Play fighting diminishes from 30- 36 days and bears no relation to which rats become dominant as adults.

Adult fighting

When adults fight, the aim is to attack – or defend – the rump. A rat may stand upright in a boxing position, he may lie belly up, or he may sidle forwards – these are all strategies to keep his rump away from his attacker. Fights are most likely to occur if a stranger is introduced to a colony.

Hissing

This is a sign of distress and will usually occur when a rat feels he is being bullied by another rat.

Squeaks and shrieks

A rat has a large repertoire of vocalisations, ranging from low to high pitch. Generally, these sounds are a sign of protest or distress – such as when a rat is being handled against his will, or if he is being groomed too forcefully by another rat. The volume and intensity will increase, depending on the degree of protest and whether the rat is actually experiencing pain.

High-pitched sounds are generally associated with pleasurable feeling, but they are of too high a frequency for us to hear.

Teeth grinding

When a rat grinds his teeth, it is known as 'bruxing' or 'chattering'. He does this to wear down his constantly-growing incisor teeth. Rats will grind their teeth when they are relaxed and contented, rather like a cat purring. It can also be a sign of stress. A rat may do this during the course of a tense interaction with another rat, when he is pain, or when he is worried.

Colours & coat types

Over a period of 100 years and more, breeders have selectively bred brown rats to create a domestic rat that comes in a wide range of colours, as well as different coat types, and new varieties are being developed all the time.

Coat types

Standard: This is the most commonly seen and it closely resembles the coat of the domestic rat's wild ancestors. It is short, smooth and glossy.

Rex: The coat is soft and curly; rex rats also have curly whiskers.

Hairless: A complete absence of hair. This variety does not thrive in cooler climates, and although it is shown in the USA (particularly in the warmer states), it is not shown and breeding is not encouraged in the UK.

Hairless rats range from having scant areas of hair to being completely naked.

Other modifications

As well as the different coat types, breeders have also developed two varieties with special features:

Tailless: Rats are born without a tail, rather like Manx cats. This may have an adverse effect, as the tail is used for balance and as a heat regulator. Tailless rats may also display spinal abnormalities, and are not shown in the UK.

Dumbo: The ears are larger, flatter and rounder, and are set on the side of the head.

Colours

The colouring of the brown rat is agouti – dark brown and banded with black hairs throughout the coat. Domestic rats come in this colour, but there are many other colours and markings to choose from, as well as selecting the coat type you prefer.

Bear in mind that some of these colours may be hard to track down unless you go to a specialist breeder.

Solid colours

This category is for rats that are one uniform colour, known as self colours. Eye colour may vary depending on the colour. Self-colours include:

Albino: White with pink eyes.

Champagne: A warm beige with pink eyes.

Black: Jet black with black eyes.

Blue: There are two blues, Russian and British. Russian is a dark, steely blue that is 'heathered' with very subtle ticking. British Blue is a solid steel blue. Both come in agouti versions and have black eyes.

Buff: An even, warm magnolia with black eyes.

Chocolate: Deep, rich chocolate brown, with black eyes.

Mink: An even mid grey/brown with black eyes.

Ivory: Pale cream with black eyes.

Marked varieties

This produces a white pattern which can be combined with any of the other colours. They include:

Berkshire: A coloured body with a white underbelly and feet, and, often, a head spot.

Badger: A coloured body, white underbelly and feet with a distinctive white blaze on the head.

Irish: A coloured body with a white triangle on the chest, white front feet and back feet white to half their length.

Hooded: A white body with a coloured head and shoulders, and a stripe extending the length of the body to the tail.

Variegated: White with colour spots or patches; the head and centre of the back is more heavily coloured.

Capped: A white body; the colour is on the head only and should not extend past the ears.

Essex: The darkest area of colour is along the spine, fading along the sides to a white underbelly with a head spot or blaze.

Chinchilla: The top colour is grey which results from intermingling of black hairs over a pearl white

Pictured:
Black Berkshire

background. White head spot or blaze.

Roan: Born solid coloured, and from 4 to 6 weeks white hairs increasingly start to intermingle to produce a roaning effect. The head has an inverted V-shaped blaze.

Squirrel: A silver blue colour runs along the back and part way down the side. The head may, or may not, be marked.

Shaded/ticked varieties

Agouti: Rich dark brown, with black hairs ticked throughout the coat. Eyes black.

Blue Agouti: Mid-blue ticking over a fawn background, with black eyes.

Platinum Agouti: Pale grey ticking over a rich cream background. Eyes red to ruby.

Cinnamon: Russet brown ticked with chocolate guard hairs, eyes black.

Topaz: Rich golden brown ticked with silver guard hairs, eyes dark ruby.

Silver fawn: Orange fawn, ticked with silver guard hairs, eyes pink.

Pictured:
Rats come in a variety of
solid colours.

Silver: Black, mink, chocolate or blue with an equal numbers of silver and non-silver guard hairs.

Pearl: Palest silver, each hair tipped with grey. Eyes black.

Argente Crème: A delicate shade of apricot, ticked with silver, shading to cream on the sides and the face.

Himalayan: White with dark sepia points on the nose and feet. The eyes may be black or ruby.

Siamese: Medium beige body colour with dark sepia points. The eyes may be black or ruby.

Burmese: The body is a rich mid-brown with darker points. The eyes are black.

Blue Point Siamese: The body is silver beige, shading into blue at the back and hindquarters. The points are deep blue and the eyes are ruby or black.

Pictured:
Siamese Dumbo.
The more exotic pet rats
come in marked and
shaded varieties.

Sourcing a
pet rat

Sourcing a pet rat

When you have made the decision to welcome pet rats into your family, the next step is to find a reputable source where you can be confident that the rats you buy are healthy and have been given a good start in life.

Pet stores

Many pet stores sell pet rats – although you are unlikely to find the more exotic varieties. The colours most widely available are agouti, black, mink, champagne and albino.

Before you make a purchase, check out the pet store to ensure the animals are kept in clean, hygienic conditions. Due to their early sexual maturity, bucks and does should always be kept in separate cages. Talk to members of staff and find out if they are knowledgeable and can give expert advice.

Pictured:
When you buy a rat, do your homework and find a reputable source.

Remember, a rat should not be sold under six weeks of age. Ideally, he should be between six and 10 weeks, which will give him the best chance of settling into a new home and forming a bond with his human owner.

Specialist breeders

If you have ambitions to show your rat, or you are keen to have a particular variety, you will need to go to a breeder who specialises in producing rats of this type. The best plan is to contact your national rat club for details of rat clubs in your area. The secretary of a local club will be able to put you in touch with specialist breeders near you.

Rescue rats

Unfortunately there are always rats needing to be rehomed, often through no fault of their own. Generally, this is due to force of circumstance – moving home, changing jobs, marital breakdown – and, all too often, rats are given up when children lose interest in their pets.

Obviously, the rat or rats you adopt will be older, and they may not have had as much handling as they need. However, with time and patience, this can be rectified, although some previous experience with rats is helpful.

Pictured:
Silver Fawn.
If you plan to show your rat you will need to go to a specialist breeder.

Local rat clubs will give you details of rescue organisations and there are also dedicated individuals who foster rats prior to their adoption.

How many?

How many?

Rats are highly sociable animals so you should not consider keeping a rat on his own. Although a rat will form a close bond with his human owner, he still needs the comfort and stimulation of living with his own kind.

The number of rats you get will depend on the accommodation you provide. Rats must always have sufficient space to exercise in their cage, and they also need time outside their cage where they can enjoy greater freedom.

The most important point to bear in mind is that rats are prolific breeders, so you cannot keep bucks and does together, or you will quickly be overrun! The option is to keep single sex pairs or groups, and decide if you prefer to keep bucks or does.

Buck or doe?

Domestic rats are out-going, friendly and intelligent – and this applies equally to males and females. However, a buck is considerably bigger and heavier than a doe, and will need more spacious accommodation.

Rats have their own individual personalities, but, generally, bucks are more laid back than does; they are slower moving and enjoy lazy times as well as their periods of activity.

Does are smaller and faster, and they tend to be more active and playful than bucks.

Signs of a
healthy rat

Signs of a healthy rat

When buying a rat, the most important consideration is that the animal you buy is fit and healthy. Look out for the followings signs:

Body

Firm and well-rounded. No abnormal lumps or bumps.

Coat

Clean and well groomed. Matting, particularly around the base of the tail, could indicate digestive upset.

Skin

Pink and clean on the ears and the tail.

Eyes

Bright, with no discharge.

Pictured:

Mink Dumbo

Nose

Clean, with no sign of crustiness or discharge.

Ears

Clean, with no hint of bad odour.

Feet

Nails the correct length and no sign of soreness on the pads.

Breathing

Quiet and regular with no sign of wheezing.

Behaviour

Active and alert. Lethargy could be a sign ill health; hyper activity could indicate stress.

Movement

Quick and agile, with no sign of lameness.

Setting up home

Setting up home

The accommodation you provide will depend on the number of rats you are keeping, but the golden rule is: the bigger the better. A rat should spend some time outside his cage every day, but, inevitably, he will need to spend the majority of his time in his cage. For this reason, the living quarters you provide should be the very best you can afford.

Basic cage

A basic cage, designed for all small animals, is made of wire with a plastic base. You will need to make sure that the cage you buy is big enough for adult size rats, bearing in mind that it must have sufficient height, as well as width, as rats are natural climbers. The bars of the cage must be reasonably close together to prevent escape.

The recommended cage space is two cubic feet per rat, plus an extra two cubic feet.

Multi-storey cage

These are wire cages with a number of different storeys that have plastic bases, and are inter-connected with ladders. This obviously gives your rats a more varied and interesting environment.

Wooden/homemade cage

You can buy a wooden cage, such as the type that is designed for keeping rabbits or guinea pigs, or, if you are good at DIY, you can make your own. However, do be aware that rats love to gnaw; they will gnaw anything they come across – even if it is their home they are destroying.

Siting the cage

Before you bring your rats home, you will need to decide where you are going to locate the cage. This should be in a room of even temperature, as rats will struggle to cope with extremes of heat or cold. The cage should be positioned somewhere that is free from draughts and away from direct sunlight. If you keep dogs or cats, they should not be allowed access to the room where you are keeping your rats.

Furnishing
the cage

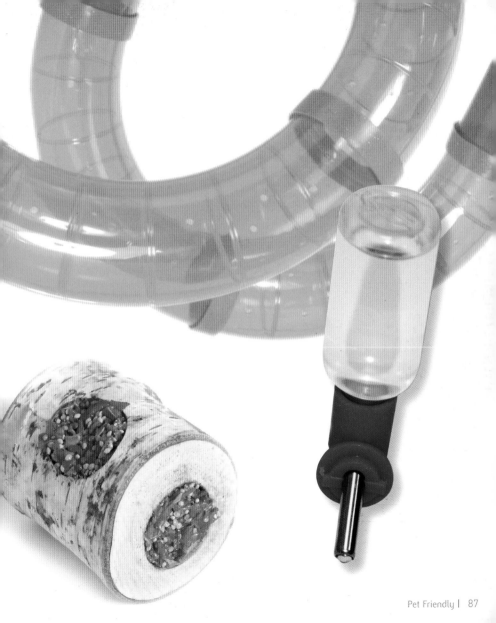

Furnishing the cage

Once you have bought a cage, you will need to equip it so that it is safe and comfortable, but also provides a stimulating environment for your rats.

Wood shavings

The base of the cage needs to be covered with a layer of wood shavings. It is best to use those manufactured for small animals, as they will be made from hard wood and will not have been treated with harmful chemicals. Some owners believe you should treat wood shavings with caution, as the phenols in them can raise liver enzymes and damage the respiratory system. Sawdust should be avoided as it can irritate a rat's eyes and nose.

Nesting material

Your rats will appreciate some nesting material in their cage to provide cosy sleeping quarters. The best type to buy is shredded paper or you can use hay. Do not use straw as this is sharp and can result in injury to a rat's eyes, nose or mouth.

You can also provide a cardboard box, which your rat can use as a nest. This will eventually need replacing as it will be gnawed.

Water bottle

A water bottle is an essential item of equipment. A gravity fed bottle, secured to the side of the cage, will ensure a constant supply of water, as long as it is topped up regularly.

Food bowl

A rat is perfectly happy to eat from the floor of his cage, but it is easier – and more hygienic – to provide food in a bowl. You will need to buy a heavy non-tip ceramic bowl which your rats cannot chew.

Playtime

You need to provide some means of exercise and mental stimulation in your rats' living quarters.

Most rats enjoy playing in an exercise wheel; it is best to provide a solid wheel so the rats cannot injure their feet. They will climb ladders and ropes, and will appreciate having platforms at different levels of the cage. Tunnels and hidey-holes are also favourites – but you must make sure that these are big enough for an adult rat.

Gnawing material is essential, and this can come in the form of wooden blocks, toilet roll tubes, and you can also use branches, from an apple tree for example, which your rats can use for gnawing and for climbing. Ensure it has not been sprayed with insecticide.

When your rats are allowed out of their cage, it is a good idea to set up an adventure playground with a variety of toys and obstacles, to provide additional stimulation. See Running Loose, page 106.

Travelling box

There are times when you need to transport your rat – you may need to take him to the vet, you may be going to a show, or you may be taking him to a friend to look after while you are on holiday.

The safest method is to use a small, plastic pet carrier or plastic aquarium, readily available at pet stores. These are safe and secure – and your rat cannot gnaw his way out!

|Feeding

Feeding

The domestic rat's ancestors survived by scavenging for food, and you will rarely find a fussy feeder among pet rats. However, as with all animals, it is important to provide a well-balanced diet, with some variety for added interest.

Dry food

Pet food manufacturers have made feeding easy for us, as the main part of the diet comes in the form of pellets, which are specially made to cater for a rat's nutritional requirements. These may also come in the form of a rodent block.

However, rats appreciate variety in their daily diet. Muesli style mixes are more interesting, or you can mix muesli style and pellets together. Pellet free rabbit food and rat pellets make a good mix, but avoid Hamster food. This is too high in fat and protein for rats.

Fresh food

Rats enjoy fresh food in their diet, and this can include vegetables, such as carrots, cabbage, swede and broccoli, fruit in the form of apples, pears, bananas and grapes, and occasional treats which can include cheese, hard-boiled egg and meat scraps.

Bear in mind that fresh food should not make up more than 10 per cent of your rat's diet.

Fibre

Hard dog biscuits and wholemeal toast provide fibre and are also good gnawing material.

Quantity

A rat will rarely refuse food so you must guard against giving him too much, which could make him obese. Generally, a domestic rat needs about 30 grams of food a day. Many owners feed in the early evening so their rats get used to waking up from their daytime sleep, and will be active during the evening, rather than saving all their energy for night-time.

Handling

Handling

Domestic rats have been selectively bred to have a more placid temperament than their wild ancestors, and there should be no hint of aggression. However, a rat is not born understanding how he should behave when interacting with people – he has to be taught.

Early lessons

The more you handle your rats, the tamer they will become, and the earlier you start, the more likely they are to form a close bond with you.

You can handle kittens in the nest from the first few days providing you know the mother well. Rats make excellent mothers and will never reject a baby, but she might nip your fingers! The breeder should start by putting a hand in the cage, and allowing the babies to sniff it and run over it. Once they are familiar with this, the breeder can start to pick them up and examine them.

By the time they are five weeks old the young rats should be happy to be handled and show no signs of panic when they are picked up.

If you want a tame rat, early handling is essential.

Arriving home

When you bring a new rat home, he has to get used to his new human family as well as a strange environment. Give him a chance to settle, and then start interactions very slowly:

- Put your hand in the cage and allow your rat to sniff it. Talk to him so that he becomes familiar with your voice and is reassured by it.

- Hold your hand very still and allow him to climb over it if he wants to investigate.

- When he has accepted your hand, offer a treat, allowing the rat to approach you and take it from your fingers.

- While the rat is nibbling reach out your hand and stroke him, very gently, along the length of his body.

- Try not to pick up your rat until he is calm and confident in your presence.

- When you do need to pick him up, slide one hand under his body and cup the other hand over his body. Never pick a rat up by his tail; it could result in serious injury.

With patience, your rat will positively enjoy interacting with you – in fact, he will be climbing all over you!

Running loose

Rats need time outside their cage to exercise and to use their brains – playing, exploring and interacting with their human family. However, this carries some degree of risk, as rats will gnaw anything they come across, such as potentially lethal electric cables – and they are also born escape artists.

Before you allow your rats to run free, you must carry out a safety check, eliminating all potential hazards and blocking possible escape routes. All members of the family should be made aware when your rats are running loose, and of course, dogs or cats must be banned.

To begin with, you may be slightly alarmed by the speed at which your rats move – this applies particularly to does. For this reason, it is a good idea to create an adventure playground (see page 90) so your rats are busily occupied, and you can keep a close check on them.

In time, your rats will become much more companionable and will tend to stay with you. Bucks, in particular, enjoy a cuddle and will even fall asleep in your lap.

Pictured:
Black rat (left) and a
Silver Fawn

Caring for
your rat

Caring for your rat

Rats are relatively low maintenance pets in terms of the care they need. But remember that you are solely responsible for them, and must always be aware of their individual needs.

Daily tasks

- Check your rats morning and evening to ensure that all is well with them.

- Clean droppings from the cage, and remove wet patches of shavings.

- Top up the water bottle – this can be done when you give your rats their evening meal.

Weekly tasks

The cage/aquarium will need a thorough clean out once a week. This will involve:

- Taking out all the cage furnishings, washing them in mild washing-up liquid and then rinsing them.

- Removing all the wood shavings, nesting material and any leftover food.

- Cleaning the cage, using a mild disinfectant made especially for cleaning small animal cages.

Individual care

Rats are fastidious creatures and keep themselves
very clean; they groom themselves – and each other
– rather like a cat does. You will not need to wash
your rat, unless he has a digestive upset and the fur
at the base of his tail becomes dirty and matted.

Show exhibitors rarely bathe their rats before a
show, unless they are white. Then it is done using
a shallow bowl of lukewarm, water, and gently
pouring water over the rat. A mild baby shampoo
should be applied to the coat, making sure it is
rinsed off thoroughly. The rat should be towel-dried,
ensuring he is completely dry before he is returned
to his cage.

Pictured:

Black Berkshire

Teeth

Rats don't need to gnaw to keep their teeth short (unlike some rodents), but they do love to do it so they will really appreciate some gnawing material. Problems may occur if the teeth are misaligned and then overgrow.

If you see your rat dribbling or showing signs of discomfort around his mouth when eating, you will need your vet to trim the teeth back into shape.

Nails

If your rat is getting enough exercise, and is running and climbing over different surfaces, his nails should wear down naturally. However, you need to keep a close check on them, as overlong nails can lead to sore feet and lameness.

If the nails have grown too long, which is more likely to happen to an elderly, less active rat, they can be trimmed using nail-clippers. Care needs to be taken as, if you cut into the quick of the nail, it will bleed. This is not only painful for the rat, it will probably put him off having his nails trimmed in future. Ask a vet or an experienced rat keeper to show you what to do – and only ever trim the tip of the nail.

Health care
for rats

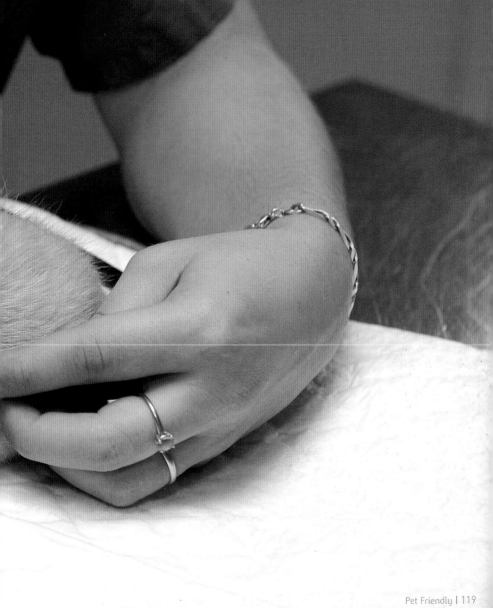

Health care
for rats

Although rats seldom live beyond two years, they are hardy animals, and with the correct care, they should experience few health problems.

Finding a vet

When you first bring rats into your family, it is a good idea to find a vet that has experience in treating rats and, ideally, has an interest in them.

Research into drugs and treatments specifically for rats is not cost effective, and so vets tend to use medication that is designed for other small animals, or even for humans. As a result, the effects of treatment can be somewhat unpredictable.

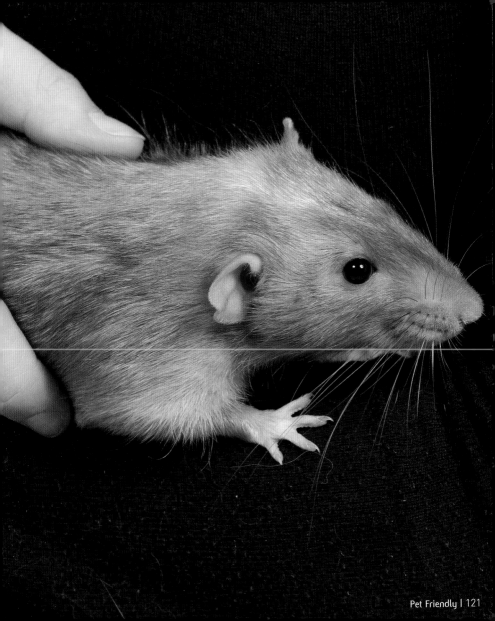

Common ailments

There are a number of ailments which can affect rats. The earlier they are spotted, and diagnosed, the better the outcome will be.

Respiratory diseases

All rats carry mycoplasma, responsible for most respiratory disease as they grow older. The first signs are sneezing, followed by wheezing and a red discharge from the nose. Treatment with antibiotics is required if sneezing is accompanied by other symptoms.

The respiratory system of the rat is delicate and easily affected.

You should also be aware that continual sneezing could be a sign of an allergy – to the wood shavings you are using, for example. If you suspect this is the case, it will be a matter of trial and error to find the cause of the allergy and then eliminate it from your rat's environment.

Diarrhoea

You will know your rat is suffering from diarrhoea if the motions are soft and light-coloured, and you see evidence of soiling around the base of the tail.

The problem is usually caused by too much green food, or a sudden change of diet. If you do need to change the dried food element of your rat's diet, this should always be done gradually, introducing a little of the new food at a time.

If you suspect too much green food is the problem, cease feeding it altogether, and wait until motions have returned to normal before re-introducing it. If the diarrhoea persists, you will need to consult a vet who may prescribe antibiotics and fluids to rehydrate your rat.

Skin problems

The two most common problems are ringworm and mites.

Ringworm is a fungal infection which causes hair loss and scaliness of the skin, usually around the head.

Mites are parasites that live on the surface of the skin or burrow underneath it. They cause itchiness, and a rat can make himself sore from scratching.

In both cases, the vet will prescribe a medicated shampoo for treatment.

Middle ear infection

A rat suffering from an infection in this part of the ear will tilt his head; he may also circle and show loss of balance. Treatment is with antibiotics, although rats that have suffered from this condition often retain a head tilt. Additional treatment with steroids may help to reduce this.

Eye problems

Discharge from the eyes may be caused by an irritation, or the result of a respiratory infection. Conjunctivitis may develop as the eyes become sore and inflamed. Treatment is usually effective with antibiotics.

When a rat is stressed, he may excrete substances called porphyrins into the tears. These are red in colour and may make the tears look blood-stained.

Cancer

This is a common problem among older rats, and may occur in many sites around the body. External tumours can be treated surgically; internal tumours are often untreatable. Most female rats will develop at least one mammam tumour as they get older. These are benign and easily removed by a vet. A high fat diet increases the risk of these lumps.

Ringtail

If rats are kept in very low humidity, the blood vessels in the tail constrict, ultimately cutting off the blood supply. This may result in gangrene in the part of the tail behind the constricted blood vessels, and that part of the tail will drop off. Fortunately, the stump usually heals without complications.

If this problem is spotted early on, and levels of humidity are increased, the condition should not deteriorate further.

Summing up

Rats are fascinating pets to keep. They are agile and athletic, which makes them entertaining to watch; they are highly intelligent with great problem-solving skills, and they have a special loyalty to their human family, which makes them unique among the small animals that are kept as pets.

Make sure you always keep your half of the bargain, and give your rats the time, care and attention that they deserve.

Pictured:
A pet rat, like this agouti, needs a combination of a well balanced diet, routine care and a stimulating environment.

Weights & measures

If you prefer your units in pounds and inches, you can use this conversion chart:

Length in inches	Length in cm	Weight in kg	Weight in lbs
1	2.5	0.5	1.1
2	5.1	0.7	1.5
3	7.6	1	2.2
4	10.2	1.5	3.3
5	12.7	2	4.4
8	20.3	3	6.6
10	25.4	4	8.8
15	38.1	5	11

Measurements rounded to 1 decimal place.